Spotting Capyvaras
In The Work Of Marc Chagall

A set of 14-liners
(but not sonnets, oh no)

Simon Williams

Indigo Dreams Publishing

First Edition: Spotting Capybaras In The Work of Marc Chagall
First published in Great Britain in 2016 by:
Indigo Dreams Publishing Ltd
24 Forest Houses
Halwill
Beaworthy
EX21 5UU
www.indigodreams.co.uk

ISBN 978-1-910834-10-7

British Library Cataloguing in Publication Data. A CIP record for this book can be obtained from the British Library.

Designed and typeset in Palatino Linotype by Indigo Dreams.
Cover design by Paula Cloonan
©2016 Paula Cloonan
Printed and bound in Great Britain by: 4edge Ltd www.4edge.co.uk

Papers used by Indigo Dreams are recyclable products made from wood grown in sustainable forests following the guidance of the Forest Stewardship Council.

Thanks to Marc Chagall for the inspiration

Acknowledgments

Nobel Gas - Templar Poetry
Spotting Capybaras in the Work of Marc Chagall - Templar Poetry
The Poet Reclining - Word Gumbo

Previous Publications

Unbroken (with Susan Taylor) - Poetry Nottingham Publications, 1979
A Weight of Small Things - Lincolnshire and Humberside Arts, 1981
Quirks - Oversteps Books, 2006
A Place Where Odd Animals Stand - Oversteps Books, 2012
He|She - Itinerant Press, 2012

CONTENTS

La Mariée...9

Spotting Capybaras In The Work Of Marc Chagall 10

Coffee..11

The Rules...12

A Useful Suggestion 13

Blues...14

Three Syllable-Counted Haiku And A Tanka................................15

Ace Fields..16

Letters Pay...17

Nobel Gas...18

FAQ...19

Flying On Titan 20

My Life 21

Sticking Pigs...22

In Vitebsk 23

Way To Go 24

Into Africa 25

Footloose 26

Images..27

The Poet Reclining 28

This sequence of poems details imaginary conversations in which the artist Marc Chagall acts as a kind of muse. To reduce a plethora of speech marks, lines are indented, instead, Narrative lines have no indent, the poet's speech is tabbed in and Chagall's speech is tabbed further.

Spotting Capybaras
In The Work Of Marc Chagall

La Mariée

(after the painting by Marc Chagall)

When I agreed to be your wife
I didn't know about the goat.
I liked your country ways and the colours
in your paintings, but I assumed
the figures were surreal, part of your art.
I didn't realise the goat would play
at our reception, though I like the cello
and he plays with a pleasing vibrato.

Then there's the learned fish;
a bream is it, perhaps a halibut?
Yes, I can see it might symbolise your work
and, yes, you did a grand job with the veil,
it's just, I'm curious – the bouquet,
is it really full of fireflies?

Spotting Capybaras In The Work Of Marc Chagall

When I saw the first, I questioned him.

Is that a capybara hiding in the bushes?

No, said Marc, It's a dog; I thought it was obvious.

But the muzzle's wrong; too deep, the jowls too big.

Ha, he said, You come from a land of bulldogs
and boxers and you say the jowls are too big.
That's the way I draw dogs.

He got up from the table and went to make a coffee.

What do you have against capybaras?

You think I have some prejudice;
perhaps I was frightened by rats in Vitebsk,
now hate all rodents, particularly the big ones?

No, I just thought you might be having a joke, an incongruity,
like a fiddler, dancing on a roof.

Coffee

Never been into café life, I said.

We sat outside, waiting for cups,

The climate doesn't encourage it
and Scoriton is more shit than skinny latte.
As a boy, I dived into the second layer,
rather than take either of the coffee crèmes.

You sell it short, said Marc, sipping his Americano.
It's not about the coffee, it's the talk,
where the ideas hiss to the top, are skimmed off.
I would grab the flavour of a fresh canvas;
Blez would swill the grounds into a poem.
We made two cups last two hours,
which is why they put us at the tables on the pavement.

I see you have marshmallows floating in your chocolate.

The Rules

Don't they say, I asked Marc,
that something has been lost with modern art,
something of the discipline, the craftsmanship?
If anything now goes, where's the graft?

You think that there are fewer rules,
because I don't use yesterday's means,
that when I put Bella by the mantelpiece,
I could have put her anywhere?
In fact, she has to be just there
or she'd not be mine as I recall,
the sun would light another piece of mat,
the horse would not be at the door.
What I have is an exchange of reins.
I soften my rules with saddle soap.

A Useful Suggestion

Why did you change your name;
was it to fit in better?

> Marc is easier to cope with, in French,
> in English. Moishe would have been
> trouble in Russia, when I went back.

> Are you happy with your names
> and why do you need three?

I don't, though I guess there was scope
to change, if I didn't like the first.
At least yours is unique. I don't know
anyone who could be Marc Chagall but you.

> I see, you want to call attention.
> Should you not do that with the poems?
> You could put a crocodile in the last line.

Blues

I've been trying to write about the sky,
but all the words for blue are tired.
It's not like paint, where you can squeeze
so many tubes and touch them together.

But I have only what the pigment makers choose.
I need to mix them up and try to tease
the shade I want with a twist of the brush.
You have everything blue to write from.

I have to do it by comparison, though,
I write 'lapis blue' or 'blue as azurite'.
You make each hue with dabs of this and that.

We both have memories;
my blue has to be how I know it was.
The contrivance is to make it now.

Three Syllable-Counted Haiku And A Tanka

Marc sat out reading
a book of Basho haiku,
a smile on his face.

You like them? I asked.

They peel off layers of voile,
a spring onion.

Is that how you paint?

The reverse – I lay it on,
but thinly, thinly.

If I painted as clean
as this man sees, I'd be blessed,
never need glasses.
He makes me laugh, oftentimes.
Is that the word, or just often?

Ace Fields

Look at the shapes of the fields, Marc.
They were where the devil dropped cards
as he flew away with sluggards who'd been playing in church.

    Ha, two of my favourites;
    cards and geometry.
    The diamond is a rhombus,
    the heart a complex equation.

That's a good line; you could be a poet.

    Ah, but I don't mean other things, only the maths.
    The skill lies in meaning all the layers.

To tell the truth, I'm not sure many of us do.
We write and sometimes see the depths much later.
I like to think it's our unconscious.

    We'll keep it secret. I do that, too.

Letters Pay

     I always wanted to design a stamp,
     a little thing, lick of spit and away.

  You'd have many fine designs for airmail.

     Ha, you're right, or for sending goats;
     just stick one between the horns,
     though letter boxes would need bigger slots.

Marc took a pen and doodled little squares,
got coloured ink and filled in his sketches.

     It's just a mechanism, after all, he mused,
     like sticking kopecks on an envelope,
     payment for a horseman, truck, a plane.
     The letter might urge you to elope,
     call you to your dying mother's bed,
     but all too often it's to pay the gas.

Nobel Gas

Marc looked up from my laptop, said

I'm concerned about the helium.

It's running low, I agreed, and cools
the super magnets in MRI scanners,
excites in lasers, stabilises rocket fuel.
Without it silicon and germanium crystals
would be hard to grow and
divers couldn't dive as deep.

Bugger that, said Marc,
Think of all the party balloons
bobbing up their silver hearts.
Think of all the fun we wouldn't have.

He took up his brush, touched
a rose on her dress in *Promenade*.

FAQ

'Who is Marc?' I hear you think.
Is he some alter ego, used to make
the possibility of dialogue, conversation?
Is he really Chagall? Does he have
any biographical provenance?
Why does he keep popping
into these reconstructions?

I will ask him, next time I meet him.
I will question him closely, though
he is notoriously evasive, preferring
to sit and paint his floating people,
his semi-rustic memories, his dogs
I take as capybaras – *see previous poem*.
Infuriatingly, he will probably just smile.

Flying On Titan

Saturn's moon, Titan, has a very thick atmosphere,
coupled with very low gravity. In fact, it is said that
human beings could fly simply by flapping their
arms about.

> I want to fly like that, said Marc, not have to wait
> for angel wings, just press up like a ballerina and go...

You'd have to go to Titan and it's
pretty murky there, I said.

> You mock me, but wouldn't you
> want to fly like that?

Of course, but it's the stuff of dreams.
A space suit would spoil the experience.

> I can see that, said Marc, but what if you could
> make suits like dungarees or pleated dresses

> and what if the sky were the colour of blue-black ink
> and what if we could take deep breaths

> and flap
> and soar?

My Life
(the title of Chagall's early autobiography)

You write these poems, said Mark,
some of which I like, and include me,
but never mention my Jewishness.

I've read your book, I said, You always
seem to be running away from it.

Not at all; it makes me and my painting.

But you're more than synagogues,
graveyards and black beards.

These are just the trappings.
Look at my mother and weep with me.

Is there a fee for this guidance,
like you paid your first maestro?

No, it's all free. I'm like a ghost;
just don't forget to note it down.

Sticking Pigs

So, what did you do for fun as a boy in Vitebsk?

Ah, we kicked a ball about and hunted wild pig.

You liked football? I wouldn't have guessed.

More like your rugby – pick it up and run.

And the pigs, were they wild boar?

Not so big, they were like small dogs
but faster, less easy to catch.

About the size of capybaras?

You and your rodents – get down to the zoo.
There were no capybaras in Russia, still none,
but you have the size of the pigs quite well.
We hunted them with sticks, Rarely caught a one,

but when we did, we had fine pork; a taste
none of these French sous chefs can match.

In Vitebsk

I've been here over 20 years,
but still wonder if I've settled.
I guess I've always moved a lot,
can't believe I've found home.

> You're not lucky in this; you need a home,
> even if it's only in your soul.
> I went to Paris, New York, but knew
> my home was in Belorussia, in Vitebsk.

What is home then? Just where you grew up?

> More than that, I think. It's family,
> it's the things that stick when your
> memory is empty. When you're young
> there is so much more room. That's why
> the place is still there when you're 90.

Way To Go

You had a lot of girls when you were young.
Were you quite the lothario?

> Don't go by all the names, many were just acquaintances
> or those I loved from a distance. Didn't you?

I had a few I admired, it's true, on the train to school,
but rarely did I date them, just once each.

> I did that too. Never knew, in the early days, how to kiss.

I read with interest, your first sight of Bella
and her eyes. How you knew she was your wife.

> Did that not happen to you too, not at first sight?

I don't think so. As I think back, I liked her.
We were on a course together, but it took some months
of correspondence before we met again. It was writing.

> Ah, you poets, always with a pen. Love is faster with a brush.

Into Africa

Have you ever flown?

Stepped off into air, you mean,
decided not to fall, make a mess on the pavement?
No, only in my head or with the brush.

I was thinking more conventionally;
I like the kick in the back at take-off.

Not fond of jets, much too rough.
The old propeller planes had élan,
more sedate, like swans stretching into air.
I'd like to have flown by airship,
great soap bubbles floating on the winds
down through Africa, over the Rift.
I would have painted the Serengeti;
elephants, rhinos, all humanity.

Footloose

My new boots, I said, showing them off,
like a girl with two engagement rings.

How do they fit? asked Marc, squinting,
Have they rubbed your toes off, yet?

I'm still wearing them in,
but that's the way with boots.

Boots are not made like feet, said Marc,
They have no toes to ripple,
take the motion out of walking.
They're good at protection, best
in Russian leather, but take them off
when you walk across a lawn
or by the sea, below the waterline.
Let your feet show their eloquence.

Images

I googled *Marc Chagall prints*,
looking for the one that set me off,
clicked on images and here are hundreds
in their primaries, swooping across the tiles.

    I've never seen them like that
    it's not like an exhibition, a retrospective.
    They're piled up here in collage,
    a mosaic of me.

You don't mind they're free for everyone to see?

    I've had my fun with them,
    they kept me in bread and wine,
    took me round the world. It seems
    a fair transaction, if anybody cares.
    Do you not feel this way with words?

The Poet Reclining
(after a painting by Marc Chagall)

Some years after the cow incident,
before the horse and sheep made pies
and mutton stews, he lay out in the pasture
practicing, as he had seen the great on tombs do.

Even when evening showered into mottled purple,
he was there, ballet pumps on slender feet,
louche black trousers up his elongated legs,
blue shirt reminding him of sky.

When the dew rose and the animals
stabled themselves,
he could feel his body rise,
pirouette the dawning stars.

Raising his Fedora to their whites and yellows,
he sneaked one into his jacket pocket.

Indigo Dreams Publishing Ltd
24, Forest Houses
Cookworthy Moor
Halwill
Beaworthy
Devon
EX21 5UU
www.indigodreams.co.uk